Could You Ever Live Without?

77 Poems and Other Poems.

- David Jones -

David Jones was born in 1989 in Liverpool, which is still his home. He studied English Language and Literature at the University of Liverpool, before specialising in Renaissance and Eighteenth Century Literature. He started writing at an early age, and has previously published two novels and a novella. His is also a filmmaker and musician.

For more information on the writer, visit: http://www.storydj.com or http://twitter.com/djthedavid.

ISBN-13: 978-1489524348
ISBN 10: 1489524347

The past is dead,
The future a
Dreaming prospect.
Life is now and nowhere
Else. Live, live for
Today I say, but
The moments tick
And groan, moan
With the dismal passage
Of time and I wait
Forever for what
Cannot be.

Believe me,
You are not real.
You are a dream,
A whispering fantasy,
A plot twist, a story.
Perhaps some trace
Of you shimmers in
The early morning air,
The dawn light - or
Perhaps we walk
Together in those
Moments of semi
Slumber at twilight.

Believe me,
You are not real,
But neither am I.
I am the dream of
Myself, the almighty
Fiction of I, and together
We will be forever,
Beyond this fickle
World of shifting sands
And dying reality.

It is 4am.
Your perfume is on
Everything, on me
On all the world - you
Are all around, you
Are all of my tattered
Senses and no poetry,
No song, no writing,
Nothing in the world,
Will make this better.

So many people
Become songs and poetry
But will never know:
Our world is full of the ghosts
Of unspoken words and memories.

How strange to think
Of all the world.
The deserts, the seas,
The sweeping tropical
Storms, the hurricanes,
Those never sleeping
Cities.

How strange to think
Of the cosmos.
The dying stars, the
Consuming black
Holes, the far
Flung galaxies and
The brink of reality.

How strange to think
That I sit here alone
In a room in a house
On a day of a month and
Think and think
Of you and you alone:
One person amongst
It all.

I want to feel
Everything but
I feel nothing.

I want to be everything
But I wait and wait -
And nothing.

Outside the snow
Falls and melts
And falls and melts.

I will always do
More harm
Than good.

Do not leave words unspoken.
Words are living creatures
And they will decay, rot,
Fester. They will become
A weeping sore, a gory wound,
And they will never cease
To gnaw and poison the blood
Until they are set free.

Wait for me at the end of time,
　　When the stars collide and the
　　Planets weep.

Wait for me at the end of time,
　　When the clocks smile at the
　　Long held jest, and cease.

Wait for me at the end of time,
　　When the desert is the sea and the
　　Sand is us.

Wait for me at the end of time,
　　Because it will be the beginning of us,
　　With nothing of those little days
　　And false concerns
　　To drive us apart, away from
　　Each other and ourselves.

In another life
We know each other well.
In this world
We pass by with a
Half smile of the
Inexplicable,
Some vague realization,
Perhaps, a moment of
Falling sand.
We pass and our worlds
Continue as they were,
Separated by space, time,
With entire universes
Between Us.

I do not have enough
Feeling left. You would be
Too much and I would
Wither and die, a falling
Star, a supernova, dying
Upon itself, sapped, drained,
Blazing into oblivion.

The entire world is a
Love song. The birds
To the trees, the sun
To the seas, the moon
A midnight serenade to
Slumbering fields. In
Every direction I hear
Those notes of adoration
And search for the tune,
The elusive notes to sing,
But I find myself a
Discordant part, a jarring
Cacophony so severed
And alone - unwanted
Amongst that orchestra:
The symphony of love.

The problem with
People is that
They are a novelty
And nothing more.
They come and go
And speak and smile
And walk and talk
But then they are gone
And it is you, only
You, alone with
Yourself and all
Your thoughts in
The dark of the night.

Tearing and scraping
I scratch and wrench
The sinews of my mind
As if digging.

Digging
Digging
Digging

Digging

Will yield some long buried
Truth, some treasure more
Ancient than me. A truth,
Perhaps to make all well -
The Ark, the Panacea.

Beneath that barren earth
Is just another day,
Same old, same old against
The fiction of change.

At night, alone,
I hear the whispers
Of those words
I never spoke.
As though somehow
They live without me,
Beyond me,
And whisper through
The silence of the dark.
They are the ghosts
Of what should, could
If only -

And I hear them for eternity.

Ravens caw the serenade
Of a winter's dying daylight,
Dwindling into barren earth,
Sewn with dreams below the ice
Which freeze and die for
Wanting and waiting.
Creaking through petrified air
The bird call groans and moans
It's rattle chain
It's prison grate
Upon a ruined ground.
Summer, spring, unreal:
It coughs and caws
The lie of sunlight,
The false promise of growth.
Wait and wait and wait we say
And age and age and age.
Life is but an interlude,
A momentary seeming
Beneath a raven's wing.

Why you?
You are just like any other,
Surely, and yet
The river sound comes
Calling through the trees
And I miss you more
Than anything in this
Whole wide world.

The vultures circle
Above my failing mind:
These pecking thoughts
Are carrion.
They whirl and swirl
And know very well
That I cannot,
Will not,
Sustain the
March of me.

Digging.

Our ghosts speak through the air.
Marooned in the past,
They stand together,
Smiling and laughing
That they will never be apart.

We did not see Him:
The Reaper of Time,
But He saw us.

And I sit here alone
In the cold of the night,
Of the winter night,
Of the snow fall night,
Listening to Radiohead
And wondering if
The Karma Police delivered
Me to you. But you are
Far away and I miss
You so much.
I miss the past,
Which contained
And held you tight.

The dust is gathering
Around me, I have left
Myself here for so long.
The world does not
Require me to spin,
Nor I it to live, it seems.
I am growing dusty, an
Old book, a broken skeleton
Hanging upon the ticking
Clock and hoping that
Some trace of yesterday
Will haul me back to life.

The only one who holds me
Back is me,
But he has strong arms
And I wonder if I will ever
Leave his steel clad clutches.
I am the prison warder of myself,
Who holds all the keys
To the cells of these forever
Moments, and his grip is firm.
I am the opposing army of me
Who commands the field
Long after the other enemies fall:
He will not give up.

I cannot defeat myself.
I cannot abandon me.

I will run across the world
And forget you.
I will forget you
In the Savannah sunrise.
I will forget you
On the roulette wheel
In Las Vegas.
I will forget you
Beneath the Aurora on
A freezing night.
I will forget you
In the L.A lights,
The Paris autumn,
The sunset of Nova Zemlya.

I will run across the world
But I will never out run
The specter of you,
Within, without -
And all alone
I will remember you
In the ticking of the
Clock, the creaking
Of time, in all
Of the world.

And sometimes
I just want it all
To fall into ruin.
The world, the stars,
The entire cosmos
Into a heap of nothing.
A discarded dream,
A used up plaything
All battered and bruised
And empty like me.

You cannot create
A monster and then
Condemn it. Hate
Its ugly features,
Its terrible gait.

When I look into
The mirror I do
Not see myself
But all of you
Who made me.

You cling
To my consciousness
Like a greedy ghost,
Guzzling and guzzling
My thoughts away
Until only the bare bones,
The carcass of me
Remains.

And then I see, in
The brutal light of
Honesty, that it is,
was, always you.

i cannot forget.

Late at night I hear myself,
My thoughts, a buzzing which
Only tempts and tempts,
Begging me, almost to
Believe - coaxing, promising,
And I stand upon the precipice,
Peering into the swirling chasm
At my feet, that place they might
Call maddness, insanity, sickness,
a bullet,
But it is screaming to be obeyed

and I smile and say a very final
goodbye to this world of ours.

Humpty Dumpty died.
All the lies in the
World will not rebuild him.
I am a razor
Blade away.

Like gunshots through
The night, my memories
Come tearing through
The flesh of the dark and
I see you again, hear you
As these hours bleed
Slowly to death.

Ruined by the sunrise
My eyes creak and groan
At a breaking day
In a breaking world.
Give me the night,
The night, the night,
The shadows and
The freedom of oblivion.

As an empty vessel I sail on,
As an empty vessel I sail on.

My course set, my sails secure,
As an empty vessel I sail on.

The sunset kisses my memory
Prow, the moonlight
Dances across my day dream
Decks and

As an empty vessel I sail on,
As an empty vessel I sail on.

It has been days,
Months, years perhaps,
Without you.
There is no time in this
Sphere, only the
Endless moment, the
Perpetual second when
You slid finally, easily,
Simply, inexorably away.
Words, words, words and
No more -
How easily you come
Now, you empty words,
You futile vessels who
Were so far away when I
Required but one of you.

I cannot remember how I was
Before. Or if I was at all. I
Wonder if the world was larger,
Smaller, defined or a haze. Or
If it was a world at all. Yesterday,
Before the change, seems a millennia
Ago, so far that it has vanished,
Cannot influence the now at all.
I have been trapped like this forever
And my trap has become myself. I
Wait and scheme my time away
Like some hoarder of fantasy prizes
Which me, the monster lurking in its
Cave, thinks are real, are genuine.

There is no time for me, no
Place in this world. I have decayed
And withered and hollowed. I am
The desert sandman, a skeleton of
Dust waiting impatiently for that
Cosmic breath, the whispering
Breeze, to sigh me into oblivion.

When I first met you
It was only chance,
Some random flicker
Of some random moment.
No grand plan,
No great scheme,
Just chance and chance
And chance.
It seems so strange,
Now, that such a moment,
Neither planned nor wished for,
Should live so long,
Forever, in fact and change

So much. Emperors and
Conquerors marched
On maps and compasses.
I only blunder and wander
Through life, but
Somehow I find you.

Another knight
Abandons his quest,
Throws aside his armour,
His sword, his spear
And destroys himself
Under neon lights
With alcohol and drugs.

An epitaph in 140 characters.

If only you knew
What you had inspired
That I still -
Sometimes the silent
Words speak
The loudest.

A twitching puppet,
Its strings cut, its
Movements sporadic,
Reality lies bleeding
Upon the floor -
Murdered, dying,
Dead. A powerless,
Gory mess it lies,
And in its place the
Specters of me come
Crowding in, those ghosts,
Those lives once lived,
Those days and memories
No longer vanished.
They smile and laugh,
Together at last, now
That the stubborn foe
Is slain, and together
We are our dreams.
I am myself and all of
Me. The new world
Before us, we gleefully
Return and live
Those blissful days, those
Careless summer afternoons,

And live forever
With those long vanished
People, those faces
Who were our heart and soul.

I could cry.
Who knows why?

I need no rhyme
Nor reason:
Just a nonsensical world
Of nonsensical thoughts
Ushering me towards
Nonsensical tears.

The terrible truth is that
I had forgotten how to
Be happy, and now
That you are gone I
Fear I will forget again.

Hatred, anger, pain
how I miss you,
you puppeteers
who were the symptoms
of life, whose tricks
I loathed, whose
strings tugged me this
way and that and made
me live. Now you are gone,
dead, perhaps I killed
you but all is an
unfeeling mess without
you, a valueless mess
that surely must
not be
preserved,
which surely must
fade into nothingness.

I do not trust myself.

    I have come to understand
    That I am all of delusion.

My world is not yours
Or mine, or any world at all.

    I dreamt you up, I know -
    You cannot be real.

The shimmering mist upon
The autumn fields, the frozen
Snow upon the lake on Christmas Day,
The ice, the night light wraiths in
Streetlight-empty roads.

And quite suddenly I miss you like hell.
This is ridiculous, I say, because a
Few mere moments ago you were hardly
Even a memory, forgotten entirely -
Almost, maybe, perhaps. And yet here you
Are, dragging words, kicking and screaming
From me in the middle of the night.

You are a far greater
Writer than me,
For I only write
And write and write
Of you, who does not
Need me to sustain
Or create. You are
Prolific, I merely wait
For the next words
You will never speak
And give them to poetry.

The world is just
A scattered raw material
For use; for art, creation -
Experience a mere tool
For writing.
Do not worry.
Do not miss.
Do not long.
Do not care, I tell myself again
And again - none of it
Is anything but fodder
For poetry, stories and song.
Do not feel, I say.
Create. Do not feel.
I whisper as the lie,
Perhaps once half believed
Dwindles into the night
Of reality, which is
Me
And feels everything.

You cannot create
A monster and then
Condemn it. Hate
Its ugly features,
Its terrible gait.

When I look into
The mirror I do
Not see myself
But all of you
Who made me.

And quite suddenly
I do not feel much
Like talking. Silent
And sullen I sit apart.

Asleep, awake - but
The world is far away
And there I hope
It will always stay.

You are the fuel,
The ink, the ghost
That speaks and speaks
So that I, a vessel,
No more, for you,
May write and write
And wonder at how
You could create
Such worlds.

Life's school bell rings
Again and again.
Making friends isn't hard
I say, if only you try.
But I am so tired and the
World seems far away.
None of you appear
Quite real in this daydream
Life of mine.

Who could have known
That we were the stars,
The dust of the universe,
Ageless and aging,
Whispering ourselves into
The oblivion of the cosmos.

Forgetful of the summer,
I was the winter moon -
Staring down,
Hopeless, alone,
Wondering at a far
Off world.

A sickle winter moon,
Alone above cathedral spires,
Wonders if it ever knew
Those summer nights.
Marooned amongst
Its star spun noose
It waits in echoing space
For voices that are faraway
And never will return.

A satellite searches
For life. Are we alone?
Surrounded by the
Dark of a dead universe?
I could not care
For space and time.
If earth is isolated so
Be it, for I am already
Alone, and I am
Surrounded by people
Upon this thronging planet.

I feel so keenly
All those lives which
I have lived, am living,
Perhaps, in some far
Off place beyond reason.
The rooms, the people,
The half familiar faces, the
Feelings of those worlds,
And I wonder how, why -
But they are real and I am
Here, severed, alone,
Marooned in time, far from
Myself.

I sat alone in the room
Of Dwindling Time and
Waited and wished as the
Sand fell and fell, drowning,
Always drowning, the world
Away until all was dust, a
Barren desert, a skeletal grin
Of a life, and I was the sand
Man, a carcass of myself,
Wishing, wishing for what
Could never be.

We tried, they will say.
Like a test tube specimen,
An anomaly, a broken
Machine, they will
Look back on me and
Sigh and say
"We tried.
We tried our best."

So I sit here and cry
Over the commercialization
Of everything. Life is
But a product borne
Upon a conveyor belt,
Art a currency, death a
Credit statement.

So I sit here and cry
Over the commercialization
Of everything and wonder
Whether my tears will
Be signed away and make
A healthy profit for
Somebody.

The most horrifying of sounds
Is the crash of dreams breaking
In the morning reality,
And all those voices
Who cheerfully claim
That it was inevitable.

When I look into the mirror
I see regret.
It seems as though he has done
All that I did not do,
Lived every life
That I did not live,
Spoken every word
That I did not speak,
Taken every chance
That I did not take.
He seems all knowing,
To see my every error,
My every feeble weakness;
None of which afflict him.

When I look into the mirror
I do not see myself,
But him, for he is what I
Could, should, might have -
Done, have been, if only -

He is not me.

I am regret and nothing more.

Thick with fog
The air is still.
Frost fall, night fall -
The frozen earth
Wonders if beyond
The haze
The chill
The hidden depths
Of torpid life,
Something of hope,
Of long dead summer,
Slumbers and waits.

The far off bird call
Of dwindling life
Comes screaming
Through the
Day time night
Of a dead winter's hour.
No ticking clock,
No chiming moments
Mark the none
Passage of day
To day to day to day.
Every sleeping minute.
Memory beneath the frost hewn earth,
Dreams above the snow choked sky,
All that was and all that will,
Frozen within the shortest day.

Do not abandon your dreams,
Because they are never
Truly gone. They live on in
Those secluded corners of
The mind and grow huge
With resentment, to torture
And torment their would-be
Murderer, jabbing specters
Howling and calling,
Clawing and biting in the
Dark of the night.

In the mirror
My eyes met my own, but he
Only smiled and sighed
And whispered quietly:

"It is already too late."

I want to go back
To a time before it was
Too late.

Life is a strange thing.
I tried not to over think,
Just take my chances.

I search for salvation
In the wrong place.

Seek out hope
Where it cannot be.

Your face will
Damn and ruin
Long before

it saves.

To leave you behind
Would be the summer meadows,
Forgetful of the sun,
Withering to winter.

Your heart is where you left
It, waiting patiently for
Your return as late at
Night your soul searches
And dreams of the one
It loves the very most.

Through this haze
I see you,
And through this haze
I know that you
Do not see me.
Drink more, be less.
You you you.
In another life,
Perhaps.

Forever - you are.
My moment has flown.
I lie in your wake
And hope.
Come back to me, as if
There could be another
Day. It is too late, I sigh
And smile - the end is
The end.

Heartbreak is so sweet,
The most pristine of sorrow:
Snowfall in the soul.

I was so happy yesterday:
That little day, vanished now,
A feather upon a summer
Breeze, a breath of an expiring
Season, sighing hopelessly,
Inexorably into the winter
Of today.

We both stare at the cell walls of air
Which are me, and wonder
Why once they were the feather
Light breeze of careless summer,
But are now the thoughtful iron
Of a none season which shuts out
You and all the world.

I need to sleep and dream these
Strange twilight morning feelings
Into nothingness.

I wrote
Some things, but
I do not have
The words to say
How my heart breaks
With every word
You speak.

How did this happen?
Scattered moments and
Fleeting glances
Should not be enough
To overwhelm my senses,
But the world shimmers
And threatens none existence,
Cracking at the seams
Of all that is You.

The world within me
Is a thief who never sleeps:
Stealing my real life.

I want so desperately
To care, but the universal
Grey of the world
Hardly inspires love,
Hate, anything -

And I sit and wait
For what will never be.

I have been searching for
Your purpose, why you
Are here, why you have
Wandered into my life
And why you roam
Freely and endlessly about
Those secluded boroughs of
My mind. Perhaps you
Are hope, the reason to
Fight and fight again.
Perhaps you are that
Final strike which will set
Me to running across the earth:
Running, always running.
Perhaps you are a
Dream of a dream, a
Speck of fantasy
Drifting about the world at dusk.
I have been searching for
Your purpose but I have
Been searching for you,
Always forever -

- And my feverish mind dashes
Back to sleep. In this
Semi conscious sickness
There are no worlds:
Reality, the dream, a blur
And I sleep and slumber
And return to those
Happy days,
Those long fled
Moments with you and
Know that here, only
Here will you ever be.

I close my eyes
Into the other world and
Hope never to return.

Alcohol and neon
At 3am. Your name
Tattooed across
The second sky.

I found myself
At the crossroads,
Met that long vanished
I of the past.
We stopped and stared,
Scrutinized, wondered
Until at last he spoke
And said -

The End.

The Jealous Reaper

Death had been my companion for all of my life. The figure of the Reaper had been a perpetual sight, for he was always there, always watching. At first I had feared him, shuddered at the hooded figure as I walked to school on icy winter mornings, my breath a frozen vapour, but my terror did not last long. Indeed, his presence became so familiar to me that I grew accustomed to it, I did not dread or fear him at all. Besides, he did not seem to pose any particular threat. He would never draw near, always hovering, lingering upon the edges of my vision, present yet far away; kept at a safe distance. He would stalk me if ever I happened to find myself in a crowd. I would glance behind and see him, far away but following, always following, maintaining a suitable distance between us but not allowing me to pass out of his vision. His black robes would flow and billow in the wind, his bone face would glow a stark white and his scythe was perched perpetually upon his shoulder, but beyond his ominous gait he did not seem dangerous and, as is the case with so much in life, I simply grew used to him. He no longer worried me. Perhaps he became such a habit that he was a comfort. I would sit in a restaurant and I would see him there, a few tables away, watching keenly. I would recline myself on a plane only to spot him there, mere aisles away, peering anxiously towards me. I would see him in shops, I would find him following me home at dusk, I would see him through my window, hear him shuffling about outside with the dawn chorus. In short, he was everywhere, and nothing in the world would let me out of his sight.

My life proceeded just as any life does, and at times I entirely forgot the Reaper. He never forgot me though, and sometimes his behaviour would alter, his quiet personality would change entirely. It was on such occasions that I would notice my companion afresh. Usually, he was a passive, even nervous individual, seemingly incapable of any dramatic violence or threat, but as my life continued I noted with alarming regularity moments when he flew into a veritable fury. In short, the Reaper was prone to rage if ever I seemed to be drifting away from him. I noticed this first when I was amongst friends. When we would laugh and talk, grin and cheer in the springtime sun, he would be there, no longer a quiet companion but one filled with anger. He would stamp his feet, clench his bone hands into fists of rage, writhe, even beat himself. Somehow, for his face lacked any truly defining features, his expression would transform into that of the purest fury. As I enjoyed life with my friends, he seethed and blazed to such an extent that I began to worry whether he would intervene, come flying into our group with vengeful strokes of his scythe. Fortunately, no such horror ever unfolded, and as soon as my friends had left, as soon as I was alone again and it was just the Reaper and I, he seemed perfectly calm, even content, and I could scarcely imagine him capable of such violent rage.

He was capable of it though, and he continued to suffer from terrifying fits of fury. The problem grew more acute as I passed through life. I encountered various women, some of whom I believed I loved, and we would spend hours together, walking, talking, smiling, enjoying the fact that we were happy and as one. Such times sent the Reaper spiraling into paroxysms of rage. His aggression, his sheer hatred propelled him into such a fury that I wondered whether he would annihilate himself beneath the weight of feeling, be simply obliterated. He thrashed about, screamed, kicked at the earth, swung his scythe through the air and looked as though he may dash his own bones to dust. Only when these lovers passed seamlessly out of my life as feathers upon the summer breeze would the Reaper grow calm and return to his unthreatening, unobtrusive following of me. I could not travel through life devoid of human company, though, and nor could the Reaper calm himself whenever such company arrived. Whenever I was surrounded by people, whenever I was surrounded by one person, whenever I spoke to others, whenever I even glanced at others or partook in a life which was not merely the Reaper and I, he would fly into that all too familiar frenzy.

Gradually, I came to realize what I ought to have known all along. The Reaper was jealous. The Reaper was all of envy. When it was only the two of us, alone and secluded, he would be silent, calm, so placid in fact that I almost forgot his existence entirely, but when I was with someone, anyone else, he erupted into his rage. This jealousy never eased, and the Reaper veritably tore himself apart. I could do nothing to alter the situation, and through life I passed, walking that sloping road upon which I often met others, some mere acquaintances, some friends, some far more, and each driving the Reaper to his frenzy. My road was not limitless though. I aged, I grew frail, the light faded and suddenly I truly was alone, with only the Reaper as my companion and no hope of any other company arriving in this life. The light mellowed, the mists hovered low across the Autumn fields and I experienced a dreamy softness which was not entirely of this world. Perhaps, for I was too enfeebled, too bewildered, drifting away from life, to truly understand the world around me, it was during these days of my hopeless isolation that the Reaper was happiest, the most content he had ever been.

Eventually, I came to die.

At last, he drew close to me and for one final moment, as though eager to savour the world while they still could, my senses clarified, grew sharper than they had been for years. The Reaper was beside me, he was ready to strike and I would die. I was aghast though, for he was not the imposing figure of Death, the great destroyer of worlds whom I had expected to greet me at the end. He was worn, haggard beyond belief. He struggled, hobbled towards me, laboured even to lift his scythe. In his eyes there was an exhaustion and weariness far more extreme even than mine. He was ruined. He was feeble. He was clinging on to existence. Like a battered mannequin he spoke at last, his voice quivering helplessly with the effort so that the sound was nothing more than a whisper:

"I have ruined myself in jealousy for you and now I see, now I see that my destruction was in vain, for you were always mine."

Novels by David Jones.

Lilith's Tears - A Gothic Fairytale. A Dark Romance.

Wrecked on an unchartered island, his ship and crew lost in a storm, Captain Trebane struggles to survive amongst the island's deadly community of immortals. Beset by the peculiar, dark magic that pervades the jungle, and the curse which has driven its inhabitants to savagery, Trebane discovers that, beneath the island's tropical beauty, lurks the shadow of an age old evil. Battling to rescue the woman he loves from the cathedral at the island's heart, he encounters the reclusive skeleton leader of the savages, along with the island's other strange inhabitants. As Trebane explores, he learns more of the island's curse, its connections with the Garden of Eden, its history, and the inexorable fate which tugs upon the lives of all its sinister occupants. Severed from the rest of the world, his quest culminates in a battle which will change the lives of the characters forever, and echo through all of time.

Lilith's Tears will immerse readers in the mystical world of the island. Magic and darkness pervade the landmass, with its fabled immortality and the curse that has condemned countless generations to languish there. Adventure, mystery, romance and legend - Lilith's Tears will both amaze and enchant.

"The author wasn't simply telling a story. He created, constructed and described a panorama of complex characters, actions and locations, which were carefully directed to evolve in a manner reminding me of past masters of fiction." Flying With Red Haircrow.

"Everything about this story is different than anything else you have ever read" Can't Put it Down Book Review.

The Travelling Circus of Lacrimosa - Victorian Gothic Fiction. A Coming of Age Story.

In 1899, Victorian England hovers on the brink of a new century, a new monarch, and an entirely new age. Soon, the world will be altered forever, but change is imminent on a more personal level for William Bury when he encounters a sinister, travelling circus on the edge of his town, and meets for the first time the charismatic illusionist Lacrimosa.

William will meet the circus again, experience its magic, its darkness, and face the terrifying scheme that Lacrimosa has set into motion. Plunged into the world of the performers, and forced to confront not only Lacrimosa and his troupe, but the bleak promises of the future, William uncovers the true nature of the circus, its terrifying history, and its plans for the world. As the hidden universe of Lacrimosa is uncovered, William finds himself embroiled in a struggle which will have dire repercussions for the entire world.

"Amazing Author!" Amazon Customer Review.

44065883R00053

Made in the USA
San Bernardino, CA
05 January 2017